Alfred's
INSTRUMENTAL
PLAY-ALONG
mp3 CD

Ultimate
Pop & Rock
Instrumental Solos

Arranged by Bill Galliford, Ethan Neuburg, and Tod Edmondson
Recordings produced by Dan Warner, Doug Emery, and Lee Levin.

© 2012 Alfred Music Publishing Co., Inc.
All Rights Reserved. Printed in USA.

ISBN-10: 0-7390-9490-4
ISBN-13: 978-0-7390-9490-7

No part of this book shall be reproduced, arranged, adapted, recorded, publicly performed, stored in a retrieval system, or transmitted by any means without written permission from the publisher. In order to comply with copyright laws, please apply for such written permission and/or license by contacting the publisher at alfred. com/permissions.

Alfred Cares. Contents printed on 100% recycled paper.

CONTENTS

Track 2: Demo
Track 3: Play-Along

25 OR 6 TO 4

Words and Music by
ROBERT LAMM

Moderately bright rock (♩ = 144)

molto rit.

4

Track 4: Demo
Track 5: Play-Along

21 GUNS

Words and Music by
BILLIE JOE, GREEN DAY,
DAVID BOWIE and JOHN PHILLIPS

21 Guns - 2 - 1

A WHITER SHADE OF PALE

Track 6: Demo
Track 7: Play-Along

Words and Music by
KEITH REID and GARY BROOKER

Moderately slow ♩ = 76

9 *Verse:*

mp

A Whiter Shade of Pale - 2 - 1

ALL I HAVE TO DO IS DREAM

Track 8: Demo
Track 9: Play-Along

Words and Music by
BOUDLEAUX BRYANT

Moderately (♩ = 104)

Track 10: Demo
Track 11: Play-Along

ANIMAL

Words and Music by
TIM PAGNOTTA, TYLER GLENN,
BRANDEN CAMPBELL, ELAINE DOTY
and CHRISTOPHER ALLEN

Fast rock (♩ = 144)

Animal - 3 - 1

Track 12: Demo
Track 13: Play-Along

BLUEBERRY HILL

Words and Music by
AL LEWIS, VINCENT ROSE
and LARRY STOCK

Moderately slow (♩. = 92)

BOTH SIDES, NOW

Words and Music by
JONI MITCHELL

BOULEVARD OF BROKEN DREAMS

Track 16: Demo
Track 17: Play-Along

Words by
BILLIE JOE

Music by
GREEN DAY

Moderately slow (♩ = 86)

Boulevard of Broken Dreams - 2 - 1

*A♯ = B♭

Boulevard of Broken Dreams - 2 - 2

Track 18: Demo
Track 19: Play-Along

DANCING QUEEN

Words and Music by
BENNY ANDERSSON, STIG ANDERSON
and BJORN ULVAEUS

Moderate disco beat ♩ = 102

(Tempo click)

Dancing Queen - 2 - 1

27 *Verses 2 & 3:*

37 *Chorus:*

Dancing Queen - 2 - 2

Track 20: Demo
Track 21: Play-Along

DESPERADO

Words and Music by
DON HENLEY and GLENN FREY

Desperado - 2 - 1

DON'T STOP BELIEVIN'

Words and Music by
JONATHAN CAIN, NEAL SCHON
and STEVE PERRY

Moderate rock (♩ = 120)

Don't Stop Believin' - 2 - 1

DOMINO

Words and Music by
CLAUDE KELLY, LUKASZ GOTTWALD,
MAX MARTIN, HENRY WALTER
and JESSICA CORNISH

Track 24: Demo
Track 25: Play-Along

Moderate dance rock (♩ = 120)

Domino - 2 - 1

50 Bridge:

66 Chorus:

Track 26: Demo
Track 27: Play-Along

DYNAMITE

Words and Music by
BONNIE McKEE, TAIO CRUZ,
LUKASZ GOTTWALD, MAX MARTIN
and BENJAMIN LEVIN

Moderate dance ♩ = 116

Track 28: Demo
Track 29: Play-Along

EVERYBODY TALKS

Words and Music by
TYLER GLENN and TIM PAGNOTTA

Moderately fast rock (♩ = 152)

Everybody Talks - 3 - 1

Track 30: Demo
Track 31: Play-Along

FIREWORK

Words and Music by
KATY PERRY, MIKKEL ERIKSEN,
TOR ERIK HERMANSEN, SANDY WILHELM
and ESTER DEAN

Moderate rock (♩ = 126)

cresc. poco a poco

Firework - 2 - 1

FORGET YOU

Track 32: Demo
Track 33: Play-Along

Words and Music by
CHRISTOPHER BROWN, PETER HERNANDEZ,
ARI LEVINE, PHILIP LAWRENCE
and THOMAS CALLAWAY

Moderately bright soul ($\quad$ = 126)

Forget You - 2 - 1

Track 34: Demo
Track 35: Play-Along

GIMME SOME LOVIN'

Words and Music by
STEVE WINWOOD, MUFF WINWOOD
and SPENCER DAVIS

Moderately fast rock (♩ = 144)

Track 36: Demo
Track 37: Play-Along

GO YOUR OWN WAY

Moderately bright rock (♩ = 136)

Words and Music by
LINDSEY BUCKINGHAM

Track 38: Demo
Track 39: Play-Along

GOOD TIME

Words and Music by
MATTHEW THIESSEN, BRIAN LEE
and ADAM YOUNG

Moderate dance tempo (♩ = 120)

Good Time - 2 - 1

Track 40: Demo
Track 41: Play-Along

GRENADE

Words and Music by
CLAUDE KELLY, PETER HERNANDEZ,
BRODY BROWN, PHILIP LAWRENCE,
ARI LEVINE and ANDREW WYATT

Grenade - 2 - 1

(YOUR LOVE KEEPS LIFTING ME) HIGHER AND HIGHER

Track 42: Demo
Track 43: Play-Along

Words and Music by
GARY JACKSON, CARL SMITH
and RAYNARD MINER

Fast (♩ = 184)

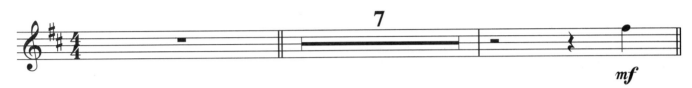

(Your Love Keeps Lifting Me) Higher and Higher - 2 - 1

(Your Love Keeps Lifting Me) Higher and Higher - 2 - 2

Track 44: Demo
Track 45: Play-Along

HOME

Words and Music by
DREW PEARSON and GREG HOLDEN

Moderately (♩ = 120)

HONKY TONK WOMEN

Words and Music by
MICK JAGGER and KEITH RICHARDS

* Percussion intro for accompaniment track.

Track 48: Demo
Track 49: Play-Along

HOTEL CALIFORNIA

Words and Music by
DON HENLEY, GLENN FREY
and DON FELDER

Hotel California - 3 - 1

25 𝄋 *Chorus:*

f

To Coda ⊕

33 *Verse 2:*

mp

44

HOW DEEP IS YOUR LOVE

Track 50: Demo
Track 51: Play-Along

Words and Music by
BARRY GIBB, MAURICE GIBB
and ROBIN GIBB

Track 52: Demo
Track 53: Play-Along

I ONLY HAVE EYES FOR YOU

Words by
AL DUBIN

Music by
HARRY WARREN

IN MY HEAD

Words and Music by
CLAUDE KELLY, JONATHAN ROTEM
and JASON DESROULEAUX

In My Head - 3 - 1

49

In My Head - 3 - 3

IN THE MIDNIGHT HOUR

Track 56: Demo
Track 57: Play-Along

Words by
WILSON PICKETT

Music by
STEVE CROPPER

Moderate R&B (♩ = 112)

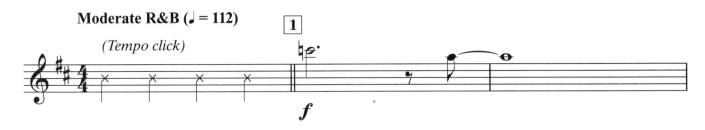

In the Midnight Hour - 2 - 1

Track 58: Demo
Track 59: Play-Along

JAR OF HEARTS

Words and Music by
DREW LAWRENCE, CHRISTINA PERRI
and BARRETT YERETSIAN

Slowly (♩ = 76)
(Tempo click)

1 *Verse 1:*

13 *Chorus:*

Jar of Hearts - 3 - 1

22 *Verse 2:*

34 *Chorus:*

43 *Bridge:*

53 *Chorus:*

mf

rall. mp

MOONDANCE

Track 60: Demo
Track 61: Play-Along

Words and Music by
VAN MORRISON

Track 62: Demo
Track 63: Play-Along

JUST A KISS

Words and Music by
CHARLES KELLEY, DAVE HAYWOOD,
HILLARY SCOTT and DALLAS DAVIDSON

Moderately slow (♩ = 72)

Just a Kiss - 2 - 1

JUST THE WAY YOU ARE (AMAZING)

Track 64: Demo
Track 65: Play-Along

Words and Music by
KHALIL WALTON, PETER HERNANDEZ,
PHILIP LAWRENCE, ARI LEVINE
and KHARI CAIN

Moderately (♩ = 112)

Just the Way You Are (Amazing) - 2 - 1

Just the Way You Are (Amazing) - 2 - 2

Track 66: Demo
Track 67: Play-Along

MR. KNOW IT ALL

Words and Music by
BRETT JAMES, ESTER DEAN,
BRIAN KENNEDY and DANTE JONES

Moderate rock (♩ = 100)

Mr. Know It All - 2 - 1

NEED YOU NOW

Words and Music by
DAVE HAYWOOD, CHARLES KELLEY,
HILLARY SCOTT and JOSH KEAR

Need You Now - 2 - 1

PART OF ME

Words and Music by
KATY PERRY, LUKASZ GOTTWALD,
MAX MARTIN and BONNIE McKEE

Medium dance tempo (♩ = 132)

Part of Me - 2 - 1

PAYPHONE

Words and Music by
WIZ KHALIFA, ADAM LEVINE,
BENJAMIN LEVIN, AMMAR MALIK,
JOHAN SCHUSTER and DANIEL OMELIO

Payphone - 2 - 1

68

(WE'RE GONNA)
ROCK AROUND THE CLOCK

Track 74: Demo
Track 75: Play-Along

Words and Music by
MAX C. FREEDMAN
and JIMMY DE KNIGHT

Moderately bright rock (♩ = 176) (♫ = ♪³♪)

(I CAN'T GET NO) SATISFACTION

Track 76: Demo
Track 77: Play-Along

Words and Music by
MICK JAGGER and KEITH RICHARDS

Moderately, driving (♩ = 132)

Track 78: Demo
Track 79: Play-Along

RHYTHM OF LOVE

Words and Music by
TIM LOPEZ

Rhythm of Love - 2 - 1

Rhythm of Love - 2 - 2

SMILE

Track 80: Demo
Track 81: Play-Along

Words and Music by
MATTHEW SHAFER, BLAIR DALY,
J.T. HARDING and JEREMY BOSE

Slow groove, half-time feel (♩ = 72)

Smile - 2 - 1

SOUL MAN

Track 82: Demo
Track 83: Play-Along

Words and Music by
ISAAC HAYES and DAVID PORTER

SUNSHINE OF YOUR LOVE

Track 84: Demo
Track 85: Play-Along

Words and Music by
JACK BRUCE, PETE BROWN
and ERIC CLAPTON

Track 86: Demo
Track 87: Play-Along

SPIRIT IN THE SKY

Words and Music by
NORMAN GREENBAUM

Moderate blues shuffle (♩ = 128)

9 Verse:

17 Chorus:

1.   2.

Spirit in the Sky - 2 - 1

THE PRAYER

Track 88: Demo
Track 89: Play-Along

Words and Music by
CAROLE BAYER SAGER and DAVID FOSTER

The Prayer - 2 - 1

Track 90: Demo
Track 91: Play-Along

WE ARE YOUNG

Words and Music by
NATE RUESS, ANDREW DOST,
JACK ANTONOFF and JEFFREY BHASKER

We Are Young - 3 - 1

WHEN A MAN LOVES A WOMAN

Track 92: Demo
Track 93: Play-Along

Words and Music by
CALVIN LEWIS and ANDREW WRIGHT

Track 94: Demo
Track 95: Play-Along

WIDE AWAKE

Words and Music by
KATY PERRY, BONNIE McKEE,
LUKASZ GOTTWALD, MAX MARTIN
and HENRY WALTER

Wide Awake - 2 - 1

YOU RAISE ME UP

Track 96: Demo
Track 97: Play-Along

Words and Music by
ROLF LOVLAND and
BRENDAN GRAHAM

YOU SEND ME

Words and Music by
SAM COOKE

Track 98: Demo
Track 99: Play-Along

PARTS OF AN ALTO SAXOPHONE AND FINGERING CHART

• When there are two fingerings given for a note, use the first one unless the alternate fingering is suggested.

• When two enharmonic notes are given together (F♯ and B♭ for example,) they sound the same pitch and are played the same way.

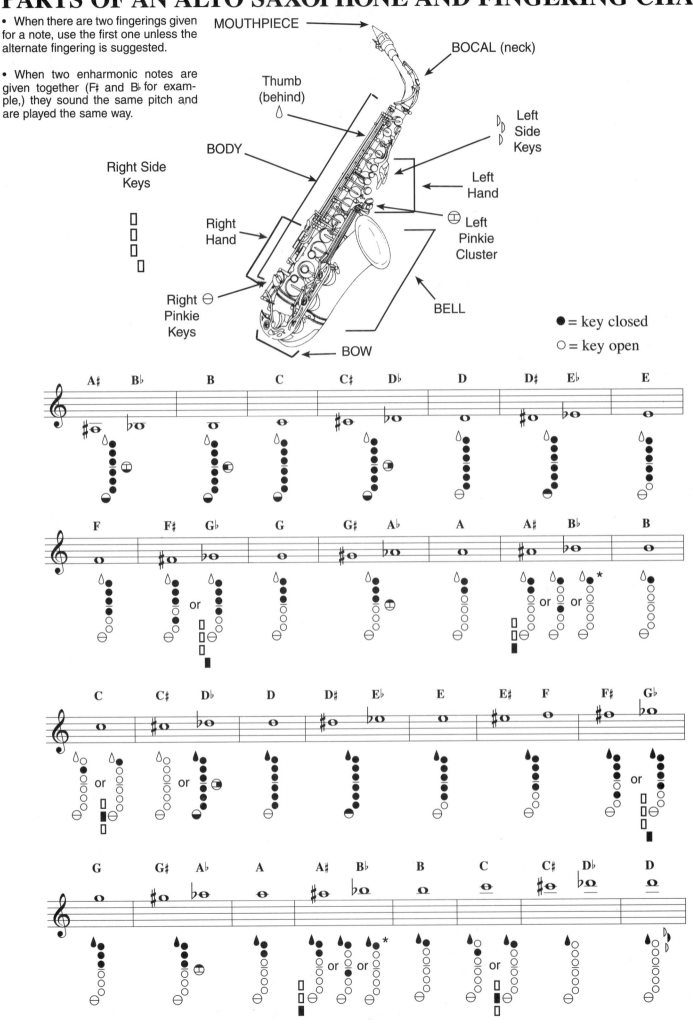

* Both pearl keys are pressed with the Left Hand 1st finger.